T0129929

Learning
Life's Lessons

SHANNON DEE WALKER

authorHOUSE®

AuthorHouse™
1663 Liberty Drive
Bloomington, IN 47403
www.authorhouse.com
Phone: 1 (800) 839-8640

Published by AuthorHouse   05/18/2015

ISBN: 978-1-5049-1030-9 (sc)
ISBN: 978-1-5049-1031-6 (e)

Library of Congress Control Number: 2015906863

Print information available on the last page.

Thank Yous

Blessed, grateful, highly favored, and so very thankful. In spite of myself, God loves me. There is nothing more powerful than the love I know he has for me and the absolute joy it brings. First, I have to thank God for not leaving me the way he found me.

I love my family and pray and hope they are blessed and protected in the Lord God's grace and his Holy Spirit. I am now at peace. I wish you nothing but the best. I pray for success, abundance, wisdom, and that you all also grow into your full potential.

I have to thank everyone who has been a part of my life, bad or good; you have helped me grow. I also wish you nothing but the best and pray for your success, abundance, wisdom, and that you all grow into your full potential as well!

Last but not least, I also have to thank my love. Without you showing me love, I would have never opened my eyes to truth.

Be True to Yourself While Making a Difference

The great American poet e e cummings said it right: "It takes courage to grow up and become who you really are." Being who you are in a society that wants to make you like everyone else is difficult. I cannot imagine trying to live as someone else. It takes courage to be yourself.

This is a collection of my life, my experiences, the lessons I learned, things that helped me to get to where I am: beauty, art, poems, quotations. Everything that combined tells my story. And I hope that by reading it, you can grow as well and be enlightened in some form.

My Story

"Slow and steady wins the race." That's what I always used to hear. But when you're younger, you don't want advice, you want to live your life. I remember my life in stories. Most of my memories deal with what house we lived in at the time and what color it was.

My parents are good people. I've always admired their strength and the sacrifices they made to give us a better life than they had. But I believe in their attempts to make things better for my brothers and me, they somehow got lost. "We were so happy poor, but when we got rich … that's when our signals got crossed and we got flipped" (—Jay-Z). It's true that when you gain more money and more worldly things, sometimes you lose the essence of what truly matters: "The main thing is to keep the main thing the main thing."

A parent is your best teacher. Most often, they attempt to keep you from making mistakes they know about (usually ones they have experienced). Even though they're not perfect, they are the vessel that brought you to this earth and are always to be honored.

My parents were jaded to a certain degree by friends and family and even the church.

Their distrust was passed along to my brothers and me. This wasn't necessarily a bad thing. I was taught to only trust in myself. But being young and unexperienced, I didn't understand their view; I hadn't dealt with this issue before. I just knew what I was told. I believe they did the best they knew how.

This, I believe, is the same way most people feel about God. I didn't understand the principles, not having much experience, and I didn't know how to have a personal relationship with him. I thought because I had done things wrong, he'd never accept me. Or I wasn't good enough. But the funny thing is, that's the whole point. True Christians are Christian because they need redemption. They admit they are not perfect and humble themselves. They live their life with respect for a higher power that they submit to. I'm not as religious as I am spiritual. I've heard a saying that religion is for people who are afraid of going to hell, while spirituality is for those who have already been there.

AUBURN

Where I'm from, my family is well known. Auburn, NY, is the home of Harriet Tubman. My family is direct descendants of her bloodline. Proud and strong would efficiently describe us. My grandmother is Harriet Tubman's oldest living relative. She travels and speaks about our family. I have always admired that. Strong women are amazing to me. The fact that my grandmother was so into history, our family history, and history in general, is the reason I wanted to study history in college. I was fascinated by those who had gone before me, people who had experienced their life, those who didn't just live, stuck and dormant, those who had gone through hurt, pain, heartache, and fears and made it, those who had a full life and overcame their circumstances, no matter what they were.

As I got older, I referred to my hometown as the black hole. It always stayed the same; the people always stayed the same. No one wanted to branch out. No one wanted to grow.

PRE-K

My earliest memory was of school. I guess this shows the importance of education in my life. My mom was my preschool teacher, so she was always around. I thoroughly enjoyed this. I loved Mom and followed her relentlessly. I was basically her little shadow. She would literally turn around and bump into me from me trailing her so closely. And that was my life: my Mommy and me.

THE CENTER

BTW Community Center was like a second home. We were always there. I was always with my family at after-school programs, free lunch and swimming in the summer, holiday dances, and block parties. There were no worries, it seemed, not like when I was older.

Kindergarten

My earliest memory is of both separation anxiety and self-consciousness. I didn't want to go to school. I didn't want to leave my mother, and I didn't want to be around strangers. Talk about the bird that doesn't want to leave the nest. I've had this issue for so long. But being the youngest and being the only girl, I was so sheltered. I was the baby, and that fact would always be a hurdle in my growth. My first day of school, I cried until Mom brought me back home. It got better as time went by, and I felt more comfortable and would actually stay at school. Every day at home, Mom would make me my favorite food. I'd have a baked potato and chocolate ice cream for dessert. Then I'd go for my half-day at school.

My father drove a tractor trailer for as long as I can remember. When I was about five years old, my Mom decided she wanted to drive with him. She left for a week or so, and during this time, my aunt watched my brothers and me. During this time, I got hurt, which was a horrible, traumatizing experience.

Busting Open My Eye

It was my turn to feed our pet gerbil named Scratch. But my brother, picking on me as usual, claimed he was going to feed him first. So playing around, we raced to the gerbil cage. I have always been clumsy, and while running, I tripped, fell, and busted my eye open on the wooden stand that the gerbil cage was on. I was rushed to the emergency room and had stitches in my eyebrow.

FLORIDA
FIRST GRADE

I barely remember first grade. We had moved to Miami, Florida, for a year. We lived right next door to my father's parents. They were a wonderful example of married life: They had been married for seventy years. My grandmother cooked a lot, and my grandfather was always washing his car. Those were my fondest memories. We had fruit trees in our backyard, lemon and bittersweet trees. My grandparents had an orange tree in theirs. My grandmother was a wonderful cook and so very kind. One day, though, she forced me to eat vegetables, and I was so upset. My grandfather called me his little movie star. I will never forget this. He was a great man. They were wonderful people.

SCRATCH DYING

During our move, we accidentally left our gerbil outside in the Florida heat, in a glass cage. When I went outside to check on him, I tapped his glass cage, and he tipped over, stiff as a board. You can imagine how traumatized I felt.

FALLING ON MY HEAD

My brother and I were playing with the kids across the fence in our backyard. I think we were not supposed to be over there. Our bright idea was to swing from the clothesline pole and jump down. To get up to the clothesline pole, we had to climb on a cinder block. When it was my turn to swing, I climbed on the block, jumped up to reach the pole, and slipped. I fell back and busted my head on the concrete block. All I remember was going black. My aunt and mother brought me to the emergency room, where I received many stitches in the back of my head. I don't remember much of anything. When we finally left the emergency room that night, the red-and-white-striped shirt I had on that day was all red, covered in blood.

We stayed in Florida for a while and then finally moved back to New York.

GENNESEE ELEMENTARY

When I came to second grade, it was obvious I didn't know what I was supposed to do. I had no idea what compound words were; I remember that vividly. I also started needing glasses to see far away.

MY FATHER LEAVES FOR A WHILE

I don't know why he left. But this was a traumatizing time. I've never asked, either, but in the back of my mind, I've always feared that this is what men do … leave. Things were going okay for us, and I still had my mother. She's such a strong woman. We stayed in a motel for a while and got to eat at the diner down the street. It felt like a vacation to me. Finally, my mother, brothers, and I moved into an apartment. I was afraid of the dark and often got to sleep in Mom's bed. This made me feel safe.

We visited my father where he lived. Valentine's Day was coming up, and I got chocolates. Another time, he brought photos that he had taken. Mom still keeps this photo up on their mantel. Another visit, my father took my brother and me to rent a movie; we rented *Hook*.

Then, after a while, my father came home. In school, I was teased, to no end. I was such a tomboy; having three older brothers, I really had no choice. But still I had a crush on a boy, and because of this, I got into fights. I made some friends and lost some friends.

Mom didn't agree with something the preacher said at church, and we stopped going to church as much.

EAST MIDDLE SCHOOL

I still was teased. I made some friends and lost some friends.

GEORGIA
MARIETTA MIDDLE SCHOOL

I was no longer teased. But I hated it here. I missed my comfort zone. The South was very different. People used words I didn't understand. My first day of school, I witnessed a fight where the girl tore out the other girl's braids, and then many of the girls in school wore them in their shoes as laces and around their wrists as bracelets. This is about the time my mother started working with my father. Along with being moved to a new place, I was also left to basically raise myself.

MARIETTA HIGH SCHOOL

I was fresh meat. My older brother was a senior, so nobody really bothered me much. My first boyfriend ever was an experience. My second boyfriend, The Hustler, was my first love. We grew so close. He was my best friend.

I began my first job at fifteen, even though my father didn't really want me to work.

Ultimately, the Hustler, and I became too close. We were so young, there was no possible way we could build a family. But he wanted to. During our several years together, I ended up having three abortions. The first time I was pregnant, I attempted suicide being so worried about what others would think. Words cannot describe the hurt, pain, guilt, and shame of these experiences.

KENNESAW STATE

It took me awhile to actually decide to go to college. I loved to learn but wasn't quite sure of what I wanted to learn. I never had the true college experience. I lived at home with my parents and commuted to school. My first love wanted us to live together, and I ended up getting an apartment so that we could. I didn't stay there, but he did, for a while.

Things happened, and we broke up. I was left to pay for the apartment by myself.

WITNESSING THE DEATH OF A PEDESTRIAN

Driving home from an event at school one night, I witnessed a horrible accident. A man crossing the street was struck by a drunk driver. He wasn't just killed on the spot, he was dismembered before my eyes.

BEING RAPED

I met a guy at a club one night while out with my cousin. We spoke on the phone, and he offered to cook me dinner. I thought this was sweet and agreed to go, as soon as school was over. I was excited throughout the day. When I got to his apartment that evening, he hadn't cooked yet but promised he would. He asked if I wanted to drink and watch a movie as I waited. I didn't really want to, but I went along.

The next thing I remember, I was feeling very drowsy. He began kissing me, and as I tried to fight him off, I blacked out. The next thing I remember was waking up in his bed with no clothes on. I had no idea what to do; I was so afraid. I got up, found my clothes, and got to the front door; I was still drowsy and not able to walk well. As I stumbled past the living room, I noticed he had friends over. I made it to my car and began to drive recklessly down the street; I finally stopped and called my brother, who came and drove me home.

The guy was never charged with anything. The police never found him. It took me a long time to trust people again, to even look at anyone or let them touch me in any way.

9-5, BEING LAID OFF

"He saw the best in me, when everybody else around could only see the worst in me."

I worked throughout college, sometimes up to three jobs at a time. After college, I was still working at my job, which I had had for close to five years, attempting to save up money for college. But then one day, I was laid off.

BANKRUPTCY

Being laid off, paying my bills got hard. I had just bought myself a new car, and I had credit cards and other responsibilities. I was in over my head.

I couldn't find a job that would pay what I was making and give me benefits. This is when I decided to follow my dreams. I went back to school and also began modeling and acting full time.

DIAGNOSED WITH DEPRESSION

I told my brother I saw an angel, who said he would take me to heaven with him. My brother brought me to a psychiatric ward, where I ended up staying for a week. They diagnosed me with psychotic depression, which later turned into manic depression and then bipolar disorder. I began to take medicine for this and see a doctor monthly.

I've battled with depression all of my life. As a child, my daddy always called me sentimental, but honestly, I knew it was more than that. I can feel other people's feelings. The feelings of others truly affect me. Most of the time, they hurt: hurt my soul, hurt my spirit. It took me a long time to realize that it was possibly sin in the world that made me feel bad. I learned what an empath was. First I had to learn people. Then when I realized what I was really looking for was inside me all along, I had to learn myself. I was never like everyone else. Things would bother me more than the average person. It wasn't until I was diagnosed with depression that I realized why that was. I'm usually content. I spend a lot of time thinking positive and being positive in an attempt to combat this. Now that I have God in my life, he sustains me. He is my rock and where I get my strength.

Mastering Life

God wasn't trying to hurt me, he was trying to get my attention. He wanted me to stop doing things I was doing and align with the path he had for me. He didn't want me to use sex, drugs, or material things to dull my pain. He wanted me to use him. He wanted my priorities to be right. He wanted me to humble myself and stop trying to control everything. I am so thankful that he forgives us. But coming to him was a journey in itself.

Sacrifices

I had to make a lot of these.

I lost people and opportunities; I lost parts of myself as I became the best version of me. If you don't love yourself, people will come along and try to teach you how to hate yourself. For a long time, I didn't understand the influence that people can have on you. I've been abused, misused, tricked, cheated, and talked about. And I've still made it through. I am so strong, stronger than I know, stronger than I can even imagine or give myself credit for.

Lust versus love, impatience versus patience. Lust is quick gratification and is often short lived. Love takes time. Lust usually beats love because most people don't know the difference.

What is love? God is love.
His definition of love:

LOVE

1 Corinthians 13 is God's definition of love. Read that scripture and memorize it! You must know what something is in order to obtain it, give it to others, as well as recognize if it is (or is not) being given to you. I used to believe I knew what love was; I found out I had no idea, til my soulmate came and showed me what true love really is. He didn't just show me with his actions or by his character; he led me to the one true source: God. When I was filled up with true love from God, I was able to give love away from a place of fullness and no longer a place of lack. Over time, the pain, hurt, depression, and fear left me completely. I have often been told that I should be a teacher; this is my attempt at making a difference.

LESSON 1: TO GET WHERE YOU'RE GOING YOU HAVE TO START WHERE YOU ARE.

From Napoleon Hill, I learned that the time will never be right; you have to just start … So here we go.

On December 14, 2008, I began my journey of change, my days of self-reflection, when I first began to try to understand myself. To understand anything, I have come to find, you must go within. That day, I wrote this in my journal:

I am gonna start living my life with me first. Its gonna be all me and others get in where they fit in. Especially relationship-wise. I gotta live 4 me. No more stress or worries period. No more overt showing of feelings or emotions. No more letting others hurt me or make me sad. No more letting anyone take advantage of me. I have 2 make a change.

I believe that was my spirit crying out for help. I needed something to change. And I had to be the one who would change things for myself. It seems as though all my life I was surrounded by dysfunction. That was all I saw and all I knew. Dysfunction seemed to be normal: drama, emotional abuse, manipulation, sarcasm, sex, drugs. I was born into sin, as we all are. God was clearly letting me know that the journey I was about to embark on was going to be different from the one I had been down in the past.

I have always believed that people who learned about me and my experiences and my life may be able to use that to better understand themselves; this has always been a vision ingrained in my being. I know that through many experiences in my life, I have been able to understand myself through others. I constantly refer to sayings, songs, books, movies … all sorts of entertainment. Entertainment, since I was a child, has been my life. It's not strange to see or hear me rambling someone's lines from a movie, and it's usually in an attempt to mimic their actual voice and demeanor, or even singing a part of a song that I just got or understood because of recent events or something. I'm not afraid to admit anything that I have experienced or know about myself. This is called transparency.

Most people are not comfortable with doing this. Many wonder why I'm so open when they can't be. And it's because I've learned that revealing yourself makes life easier. I'm not afraid to laugh at myself. Not at all. I am not afraid to make mistakes, as long as I don't keep making them. On the path to success, you will fail many times. The point is to keep going. I've had many issues. I used to curse. I had a li'l bit of an anger problem. My parents instilled values and morals in me when I was young, yet no one really raised me. I was left to fend for myself and be influenced by those around me. I love blunt/upfront people. I just love people in general, when I'm happy with what I'm learning from or through them. But when I'm not happy with what I'm learning from people, hearing me exclaim, "I hate people," should be of no surprise.

And I dig guys with cold exteriors but who are total softies when you get deeper. Cuz I'm like that. I even like people with a mean/funny assholish-type, sarcastic sense of humor. Me all the way. Don't be offended. People are energy. I constantly make up inventions for things I don't wanna do when I'm lazy or to make life easier in my mind. I pride myself on being understanding. I think it's fun to analyze people's feelings and actions and thought processes. I think I can read minds in a way, when I know someone.

People love me. No, let me start over with that. My friends who know me, know who I am and know how I am, love me. "Why do they love you?" you might ask. Why? Cuz I am real! And I never realized how I am or why I am until now. I am fully starting to understand my purpose, as in what I've been being prepared for in my life. God has a plan for you all. And believe me when I say this: He has this plan. Just cuz you don't know it or understand it doesn't mean it hasn't already been constructed. It is complex and intricate as shit. And to realize that, I am totally amazed by life, period.

So back to my purpose. Sometimes this is an issue. Many times people see me as a mirror of what they hope to be. This can go well or not. I tell people in my life what they need to hear. This might seem strange. I totally believe in Socrates's idea that the man who knows something knows that he knows nothing at all (think about that for a while). I just feel as though I have totally been put here to help the people I go through this crazy thing/journey/learning experience that I call life with. I have been put here to be a blessing. While helping them, I in turn help myself. To be a blessing to others in turn blesses you.

For me, just about every day in my life I learn something in some way. Not just in a school-type atmosphere; I read a lot, mostly about self-development. I learn from people and our involvement with each other. (I totally understand the sayings "You learn something new every day" and "You never stop learning" now.) As I get older, I am constantly attempting to master life and myself. I believe this is the path to success. Success could mean something different to any given person. To me, to be successful means to be free, wise, prosperous, healthy, happy, and able to experience it all.

So with that said, I will begin the journey of how this person came to be, in all of my complex simplicity. Oh and last, but not least, I analyze everything, sometimes way too much, but I really do, with everything that goes on. And if I'm ever overanalyzing, I expect someone to tell me I am. I expect my true friends to tell me I'm wrong, even when I don't wanna hear it. A big fault of mine is that I expect too much from people and sometimes make quick judgments. But I realize no one is perfect, and

I'm easy with compromise. So I do tend to get over things quickly. I don't dwell.

I get stuff. Like "get" it, as in truly understand things and people. Like get them for who and what they are and try to totally accept that. Some people, well, most people who don't know me might judge from my exterior. Some might let their view of me physically decipher what they think of me. And now I truly understand the saying "Don't judge a book by its cover." I think God made me pretty because he knew it'd make it easier for people to listen and feel what I say. I dunno bout y'all, but when something looks good on the outside, I'm just a li'l more inclined to try it. Lol. But however shallow that sounds and may be, it's real. Things really do happen like that. I've seen it time and time again. But just because something glitters doesn't make it gold.

I have been trained and learned to be pretty inside as well, to have substance. But my real friends know that I tell them real stuff, whether they wanna hear it or realize it or not. I am that friend you say, "Man, I want her around, cuz I know whether bad or good, she gonna just keep it real with me." And I do, sometimes to a fault. Sometimes I'm not nice about it. And sometimes, I can even be quite hurtful about what I say or how I say it. And this is usually how arguments go with me: tough love.

But the saying "Only the strongest survive" is sooo true, with me and also clearly with life, period. Real friends and real people are totally okay with the fact that learning about life and even yourself is not gonna always be fun or easy, but it will be worth it all. Growth is not easy. It hurts. A seed must be buried in the ground and rise through the dirt to get to the sunlight. And then it keeps growing into the air.

I make people think, like truly think about things, concepts, events, songs (and my friends know I'm good for pointing out music; it's a totally tremendous part of my life, but I'll get to that later), and actions and consequences ... life, period. I keep people on their toes (prolly why my hustlin' homies think I'm a cool chick, which I often hear). I think different, and I'm not afraid to laugh at myself, and that might intimidate people who don't understand how someone could think like that. People who don't understand either hate others who do or are drawn to them. People do fear what they can't explain. I fear nothing. Anything I did fear, I overcame. Not everything that happens is gonna be good. Life is complex and hard. And when you live, I mean really live, you realize that more and more.

Sometimes people get mad cuz they don't wanna hear what I say. Someone told me today it's hard to accept something you don't want to accept, and it truly is. I've said things to people and have not talked to them for months cuz of it. I've had someone hurt me, and I've gone months without even acknowledging their existence. And when they come back into my life at some point in time, which always happens to me, they usually confide in me I was totally right in what I said or what I did. Or they say that I've made them a better person. And they see me totally differently than they thought I was. Well, mostly … I'm not perfect. I just don't hide who I am. I am an open book. I always tell people. I don't lie. But most people do lie and try hard to hide their real selves from people.

I am extremely comfortable with who and what I am. On so many levels, that can be confusing to anyone my age who is still learning who and what they are and what is and isn't important in life. I believe that maturity cannot be measured by age. It comes from a combination of experiences, as well as morals and values that are instilled in you. Through my experiences, I've pretty much set my morals and values in stone, which many people, with how society is today, do not understand, cuz they didn't get these ideas instilled into them by their mothers and fathers. (I can go on for days about the sadness of kids having kids and how I feel about bad parenting.)

My parents are who made me, my roots, totally how I began to grow. They raised me right. I commend them fully. They are the shit. Total superheroes in my eyes. But like I said, I am learning, exactly as those in my life are. I just grow through people (meaning with their help). I love that about my life, absolutely love it! It is hard as hell to deal with while in the moment … but when I look at the big picture, I realize what I went through was exactly what I needed to be going through at that time in my life.

I've had people tell me, "Oh, you're too sensitive." Thanks, Dad, for attempting to toughen me up. I will always love you for that (and this is closer than some people get the opportunity to see me, cuz I definitely do not show all my facets to everyone). I am a diamond, with different colors and facets. Some of you may think I'm a plain shape. That's just flat chillin' there on a flat piece of paper. But the closer you are to me, you realize that I have sooo many different sides and angles. And that, I think, is my blessing. I hope to one day find that person in life I can grow with who will see all my facets in the sunlight and just be okay with them, whether they're flawed or not. That right there, I believe, is true love, like that unconditional love that God wants for us. Or maybe I have found them and just don't realize that is who they are supposed to be yet in my life. Mmmm, who knows? :) Life is crazy. It could happen.

I've always known I was meant for great things. Always. I just never was sure quite what those great things were. I have on countless occasions told close friends, "I'm supposed to be rich," like I always knew I was meant for the good life (*She Got Her Own* plays in the background as my theme song). I always have been faceted. I've had the weirdest experiences in different types of attitudes, clothing, music, movies, people I hang out with … everything. I don't just grow one way, horizontally or vertically; I expand, in all angles.

I am genuine; not everyone understands that. I come across as being arrogant or full of myself to those who don't really know me. That is just because I know what I want. Supposedly New Yorkers have a swag that says, "I'm better than you." But my close friends know that is in no way true. I actually have had problems with many insecurities. And I have no problem admitting that. I totally own the idea that I am nowhere near perfect. But I think imperfections are sexy, along with character and integrity, especially when confidence is also involved.

I love strong, and I have claimed to be in love with plenty of guys throughout my life. Well, not really plenty, but my fair share. And I have truly loved them all. But through understanding that I am still learning and still experiencing, I totally see how and why I felt the way I did when I did. But a very small few have actually gotten to remain close to me. I can't wait for the one who stays close for the rest of my time on this earth.

Starting out as a young girl, I was very confused. I didn't know how to open up, but few people would believe that about me. I had not totally bloomed yet. When I was young, my mom used to say I could only have one friend at a time. And maybe that was true. I could only concentrate on one person at a time, cuz I thought friendship meant I had one best friend, and everyone else was basically enemies. Believe it or not, I lived with this idea for a very long time. Lol! Me and my one best friend against the world. But don't let my best friend do something I didn't agree with or something that hurt me; I'd drop them and find another best friend.

Slowly, and very slowly, might I add, I came to the idea that friends can have degrees of closeness. It's not total bipolar sides of friendship. People will come into your life, and people will go. And now I am to the point where I don't have many close friends. I do have people in life where I know who I should go to when I wanna hear what I need to hear or do what I need to do. And this may sound quite selfish or manipulative in a way; maybe.

But I will explain why that's not necessarily a bad thing (unless it's overused). Everyone is selfish and manipulative in their own way. Everyone wants to be right. And altercations, problems, fights, all types of negative vibes come from people trying to push their idea of right onto another person. When you're cool, you understand this concept and compromise and accept it. But when heads butt, it's cuz you cannot make this sacrifice and compromise. And this is clearly gonna happen throughout life. Maybe in some cases not as severely as others, but it will happen. That is life. That is life. Those who understand that, understand the saying "The world does not revolve around you." No, if you think about it, you actually revolve around the world and zoom in to match with people at different times, angles, places, and so on. Selflessness, I believe, is one of the best characteristics a person could ever have. I try and live my life sticking to that idea.

The important things in my life, I believe, show, express, and explain (or at least give a glimpse into) who and what I am, and why I am how I am. My favorite color is yellow. It has been since I was about ten, when purple used to be number one. Lol. I used to hate pink, only cuz my surroundings made me not wanna be labeled as one thing. Pink was such a girl color to my young mind, and I didn't wanna be just girly. I was so many other things. A big part of that was being a tomboy. Hey, my best friend was my older brother; who else was I supposed to be like? Lol. And I hated bows and sparkles and anything too girly. My mom used to cut 'em off my shoes and dresses. She hated them too; guess that's where I acquired that idea. They've grown on me now, though. Lol. But back to yellow: It's my favorite color. And when people ask why, I always say, "Cuz it makes me happy." It makes me think of sunshine, and sunshine makes me happy. And why is this important, you might wonder. Well, I have a problem with depression. This may be surprising to those who don't know me. I've always known it. Never been diagnosed, but when you know something about yourself, you truly know it. I'm just not afraid to admit it. So when I realized that I have depression problems and couldn't live life being sad all the time (cuz I do tend to be seasonally depressive), I thought, What makes myself happy? Like all the time, no matter what? Sunshine! It shows warmth and light; it just makes me have that tingly, everything is wonderful, it's gonna be a wonderful day feeling that I love.

So during my preteens, yellow became my favorite color. I painted my room yellow and spent a lot of time in my room. It made me feel safe. "It doesn't take a whole day to recognize sunshine." I love that bar from Common. Actually the whole song, so true. It doesn't. And if it does take you a long time to come to the realization that something is good or makes you happy, that's something you personally need to work on. It shouldn't. Nothing lasts forever. Be grateful for the little things.

Color association is a big part of my life. In my family, we don't memorize the addresses of places where we have lived, we mostly remember the color of the house. It's funny when you think about it, but we've never lived in the same colored house more than once. As I grew up, it was the yellow house, brown house, and so on. And each house holds great memories. If the walls could talk at any of these places, they would blabber on about how I came to be.

It's crazy how when you're with someone, they can make you insecure. You can be the baddest, coolest chick ever, but no matter what, there's always that one person who makes you act so lame, your kryptonite, totally breaks you down. And the funny part is, most of the time, they don't even know what it is they do to you.

I've wasted a lot of time in my life, instead of using it to its full advantage. I've spent countless hours held down by emotions and people for no reason. I've been sad and depressed for days that lead to no type of progress in my life whatsoever. Oftentimes, my emotions totally control me. I have to learn how to be the one to control them. Every second spent being sad is a second wasted that had the potential for happiness. Truthfully, nothing is ever wasted, especially an experience. The point is to learn something from everything you go through.

I am thoughtful, pensive, and very analytical. I am learning to be patient. But I believe God made me with the foundation of betterment and had me learn, through my experiences, about the building blocks that constructed my skyscraper of knowledge, love, and strength, so that I can be all that I am meant to be.

I've spent a lot of time being interested in others, trying to get to know others, molding to others and their needs and wants, instead of focusing on me. I believe many young women in my time focus too much on others and not themselves. Many women don't even know themselves: their likes, dislikes, how they are, how they act. They haven't truly figured out who they are. And I think this is such a shame. I am just finding myself. Who I am, what I want and need, and what I want out of life. We are thrown into this world and life with no instructions. And role models are few and far between. What we see and strive to be is the prettiest girl who everyone wants. But trust me, that is not the best you can be. I searched for love out in the world; I finally found it when I started searching inside of myself. Not every person you meet of the opposite sex is a potential mate. Some people just enter your life for a season or a reason to teach you a little about yourself.

LESSON 2: LIFE IS CHOICES AND DECISIONS.

Throughout our life, we are forced to make choices. Whether good or bad, the choices we make are our own personal decisions we must live with. Sometimes, the decisions we make are easy, and sometimes, the decisions we make are very hard. Sometimes, we regret the decisions we make. Each choice and decision you make moves you along on your journey. I believe there are no mistakes in life, because you learn from everything that you do. By acting, you are doing a good thing. To move, you must act, although you should always make sure your choices and decisions are pushing you in the direction you want to go. Try your best to let your choices and decisions make you better and take you forward.

LESSON 3: EVERYTHING HAPPENS FOR A REASON.

When you are not afraid and trust God beyond what you believe you are capable of doing, it pleases him.

I've always been called a hopeless romantic. And while I do believe in romance, that's not what I am. I am simply a believer. I believe in a higher power, in universal truths, in people, in good, but most of all, I believe in love. I don't have everything figured out; I'm still growing and learning, but I have faith that everything I experience will be everything I need to make myself the best version of me I can be.

Being pretty and kind, it seemed as though the wrong people always wanted to take advantage of me. People would often take my kindness as a weakness, my innocence as naivety. Being a good person, I believed in the good in people. I guess that's the mind-set you get when you come from a small town.

When I figured out that being the best me I could be was the only way to bring me closer to God, make me strong, and make it possible to attract the good things into my life, personal development became a passion.

God sure is a comedian. This is what I often think as I experience the trials and tribulations he places on me to shape me into the person I am meant to be, the lessons I need to learn to build me into my character.

My life has been quite the adventure: peaks and valleys, ups and downs, highs and lows, hurts and pains, but I was holding onto the pain instead of giving it to God and leaving it with him. Instead of learning from it and moving on, I was carrying it with me. This, I realized after some time, slows you down. You can't carry extra baggage. I realized I had to give it all over to the lord and stop attempting to keep taking it back. Pain and hurt, trials and experiences have a purpose. Their purpose is not to harm you but to help you grow stronger. You must grow bigger than what you experience so you can grow into your full potential. At each level, you experience things; you must get better so you can keep moving along on your journey. I had to be strong and realize that once he takes your sins, they are gone. Once you give God your sins, he lets you know you have already been forgiven. Jesus died for our sins.

The bad part is the enemy will replay your sins in your mind. He wants you to feel bad and feel guilty. He doesn't want you to grow to your full potential. He doesn't want you to be happy because he isn't happy.

I prayed that Jesus forgives me and protects and covers me in his blood. He cleared all my pain away. I am now peaceful and can enter his kingdom when the time comes. I had to be healed from my pain. I had to let go of everything that was not good for me. This is something I do daily: forgive others and forgive myself.

LESSON 4: YOU NEVER KNOW WHO WILL BE YOUR TEACHER.

You should never be sad because something ends, you should be happy that it began and you were allowed to have that experience.

You should be grateful for everything that comes into your life to give you an experience, as it has been sent to train you or help you grow.

Negative people let you see what you don't want to become. They treat you how you don't want to be treated and show you what you don't deserve. You must embrace the revelation, work on being better than that, and let it go.

God's gift to you is the ability to overcome self. Everyone I encountered taught me a lesson. And that is exactly how your journey should go. You should learn something *every* day. Whether it's at school, at work, in your own personal studies, from someone. To grow, you must learn. Sometimes, what you learn changes you, and you will become different and think different. That is fine. Just keep moving forward with your truth. God does not waste experiences. Everything I've experienced will hopefully help someone going through what I have gone through. I hope that it will prevent someone from suffering through the same experiences. You are not alone.

I pray it will give someone hope that despite their conditions, shortcomings, circumstances, God can still use them, that they too are a special, wonderfully made masterpiece, and that they have a purpose. Throughout my journey, I have learned from many people. And my attempt is to give credit to everyone who has ever helped me learn something in my life (whether good or bad).

LESSON 5: EVEN A BEAUTIFUL FLOWER MUST GROW FROM THE DIRT.

The candy-coated peach: Atlanta vs. New York

In the small town where I'm from, everyone knows everyone else. People are more important than things. I guess that's because all we had were people; we didn't have many things. The town where I was born is full of my family. When I moved to "the Hollywood of the South," I found out life was a bit more superficial for most. I found out how evil some people truly are. I experienced things I would never wish on my worst enemy. But through it all, I've grown. I'm better, stronger, wiser. I now have a story I can share. God has definitely turned my mess into a message.

From a young age, I was conflicted with wanting attention but not wanting too much. I was so confused. I was always told that I couldn't do this or couldn't do that. I was shy and timid yet always the overachiever. I would shift back and forth from wanting so hard to prove myself and make others proud, to just not caring and wanting to give up. My whole life, I've been in search of what I didn't know: of myself, I thought; what I like, what I don't like, who I really am. All I ever wanted was to be loved. I found out I was really in search of God. He was what was missing from my life. It took me a long time to figure that out. Despite my ignorance, I also had a fear that was instilled in me since childhood.

When I was younger, I was never the prettiest. I was never the one with a lot of money. I was never the luckiest. I never had the nice, fancy stuff. I wasn't the smartest. I wasn't talented. I wasn't athletic. I wasn't funny. I wasn't popular. I wasn't anything special. I had such low self-esteem. I was a shy, awkward little girl who was self-conscious and insecure. I was teased relentlessly for how I looked: my hair, my clothes, my big eyes, my mustache (kids said I had one) and the mole in my nose they claimed was a booger. I was teased; I was picked on. And the worst of these things was I was introduced to sex, way too early.

As I grew up, that all changed. I learned to master my fears and turn my weaknesses into strengths. I taught myself how to become a jack of all trades. God had given me great potential, which I hadn't even dreamed of tapping into. He gave me many talents and gifts to use, but I was blind to the fact. Now I'm happy and fulfilled and following my dreams. I've had to overcome a lot of hardships, which no one has any idea about, but I still have to deal with the hate and jealousy of those who have not overcome their hardships or who stopped following their own dreams.

Being successful comes with a price; you lose people. The successful journey is a solo one. You can't carry people on your back as you climb the mountain. You can't help anyone get there. If they can't get there alone, they weren't meant to make it. Lao Tzu said it best: "Give a man a fish and you feed him for a day. Teach him how to fish and you feed him for a lifetime." This is my attempt at teaching whoever wants to learn how to fish. I've only ever been fishing once, but personal development is something I pride myself on. Get your vision out of your head, and you can make it all come true. When you're following God and living in your purpose, all the good things you pray for will find you. All you have to do is trust in him and trust that everything he does is for your good. Whether it is a bad or good experience, you will grow from it. Everyone falls short. But that is no excuse to be stagnant.

LESSON 6: IF HE WANTS TO LEAVE, LET HIM.

The Heartbreaker

Freshman year in high school is the worst, especially if you're cute. All the older guys want to hit on you, of course, cuz you're fresh meat, something new and different. And that's what young boys want: someone new and different to corrupt. So me, being a young, naïve girl fell for an older boy, my first. The Heartbreaker was three years older than me, the same age as my brother; he actually was a friend of his. My brother never wanted us to date, prolly cuz he knew what kinda person he was, not someone who deserved his innocent li'l sister. But I, not understanding that, went for it anyways. We spent all our time together (after school, of course). I would take a cab to his home and hang out with him. I was so in love … and then he broke my heart. It took awhile, but my next guy came and saved me. It wasn't hard to move on.

LESSON 7: WHEN HE NEEDS YOU, BE THERE.

The Hustler

He used to say hello to me every day. Every single day. "Hey sexy," or "Hey light skinned." I mean, this was high school, and his locker was behind mine, so of course that was easy access. But this was different, way different from any attention I was used to. Sometimes I'd look in my locker mirror at him, just to admire him a li'l bit. He caught my attention … and this was not an easy feat. He wouldn't usually see me looking, but a few times he would wink or nod his head in appreciation. This would make me smile. It would actually make me blush. I had a boyfriend, who wasn't treating me very well anyways, but still, it wasn't right to be interested in someone else. But he was my ideal guy: light skinned, with a slight New York accent. One day, he went so far as to say, "Man, I can't go one day without saying hey to you; I must love you or something."

And that was the beginning of me wanting something new, wanting better for myself. He exuded confidence. He had such an aura of self-awareness. It was really nice. I'd never seen anything like it, being sixteen and not really knowing who or what I was myself. He seemed so sure of himself, so sure about life. I wanted to be like that. I gave him my number, and we began to talk after school. We would talk about everything and anything. It was the highlight of my days. The Heartbreaker was doing what he did: breaking my heart, so this was a pleasant time-passer. I found out the Heartbreaker was still seeing his ex, and even though it hurt badly, I didn't care as much as I would have if I had still been totally invested in him. Clearly, I wasn't.

The hellos every day at school made my day, and the talks after school made my evening. Weekends were hard, cuz I didn't get to see my new crush. One day at school after his gym class, he was a li'l bit upset. He had lost over a hundred dollars. That was strange to me. And I not having had a hundred dollars to my name could not understand why he wasn't more angry. I suggested he report it or something, and he quickly swatted that idea away. I didn't get it. That was a lot of money. And my naïve mind, which knew nothing about anything, just couldn't understand. I was nowhere near a part of that type of lifestyle this boy was involved in. But this is where I learned how to be street savvy, which is something I would need throughout my life.

And from that day forward, I knew he was the hustler. The hustler was the perfect package. He was smart, funny, loyal, dedicated, and most of all he loved me. If the definition of a real relationship is where a man protects you and provides for you, this is my example of the realest relationship I ever had. He set the bar. He wanted everyone to know I was his. He was so proud of our relationship. And I was so proud that someone wanted me in that way. His love gave me confidence and courage. We grew together for a long time. So long even now I know we'll never truly be disconnected.

After a while, times got hard. In high school and college, you're growing and changing; he wouldn't let me go at my own pace. He wanted to force me to be what he wanted. I wasn't ready … and he wouldn't wait for me. That's when the love started to fade. Not exactly fade, but things ended.

LESSON 8: SOME GUYS JUST LIKE TO PLAY GAMES.

The Dopeboy

He was Mr. Popular. Strong and attractive; there was just something about him. I really liked him. But really it was just because he was something new. He reminded me of the Hustler, just a newer version. This is where the 80/20 rule comes into play. It is said that in a healthy relationship you get 80% of what you want. But most are constantly searching for that missing 20%. That 20% that is wrong is said to be work you need to do on yourself. Not something your partner really needs to change. I was just an option to him, not even number one. He just really wanted to compete with the Hustler.

Mr. B-Ball

Mr. Popular again, but in the sports field. I didn't play sports but still thought he was so interesting. But once again, I was only an option to him.

LESSON 9: EMOTIONALLY UNAVAILABLE MEANS UNAVAILABLE.

The Baby's Daddy

He wasn't really ready for life. I was just an intermediate person to pass the time while he got there.

Mr. Grown Man

He was so together, responsible, and grown. I admired him. He was my sordid idea of what a husband should be, in that "you go to college to find a husband" way. But honestly, I wasn't ready for that responsibility. And he wasn't really serious.

The Disbeliever

He had emotional issues. And I guess by then, so did I. He wanted love, and then he didn't. He was angry, and then he wasn't. He'd been hurt before.

The Liar

He wasn't ready to let go of the single life. But instead of being honest about it, all he did was lie about what was going on. He said he wanted to be serious, but then he really didn't.

Mr. Devil in Disguise

He only wanted me to have me. But he was a liar and a cheater and wasn't right within. He'd woo me, but all the while he had a girlfriend. Lust was the game.

LESSON 10: DON'T LET HIS INSECURITIES MAKE YOU INSECURE.

People who don't know themselves are fascinated by those who do. Those who don't love themselves are the worst people to fall in love with.

The Superstar

He really tried to make me better. But things between us weren't right. He was the closest thing to love since the Hustler. He cared for me, and I cared for him tremendously, but we both knew we weren't right for each other. We were just scared to let go and not be safe and secure.

Lesson 11: There is no competition.

Mr. Constellation

Mr. Constellation was like a fairy tale, a beautiful fairy tale that became a nightmare. During my clubbin' days, I would see him all the time, out and about. There was somethin' about him. His eyes showed the pain from his soul. He intrigued me. When we'd see each other, we would just stare. We'd never even talk. And he never spoke to me, prolly cuz I looked so unapproachable. He claimed later on he wasn't gonna take the blow to his ego and risk getting turned down like other dudes did when they approached me. And it was true, I did turn down a lot of dudes, but I wasn't the type of girl to put up with the bullshit. I'd heard it all before. This meant he liked easy prey. I shoulda taken that into consideration and never thought about him again.

It took awhile for us to get in contact with each other. And I made the first move, cuz I'm not scared to go after what I want. But when I get what I want, I really need to learn to handle it, more like control myself. So when I finally found him on Facebook, I didn't hesitate to hit him up. A quick "Hey, I see you out all the time and we always look at each other and never speak." He replied, and we chatted back and forth for a while. He saw I was in a relationship and asked how it was going. I told him it wasn't going very well despite the love I had for the guy. He replied that he really liked a girl and was trying to figure out if he wanted to make her his girlfriend. I respected that. I guess he respected my situation too. He asked for my number and said maybe we could be friends and hang out sometimes. I gave him my number but let him know chilling would probably not happen, cuz I was in a relationship. I guess he respected that, cuz he never did call.

The Superstar, who clearly had my password, read our conversations and was angry about it. Angry that I gave my number out and would want to talk to someone else when we were together. But he was talking to all types of females, and I knew. Why shouldn't I keep my options open? Why should I put my all into someone who clearly wasn't putting their all into me?

Two weeks went by, and I still hadn't heard from Mr. Constellation. This kind of bothered me, cuz I didn't usually give my number out, and that was a lot of effort on my part, especially because I got in trouble with the Superstar for doing it. And I couldn't even get a call? Really made me angry, but I didn't say anything to him about it.

So one night, I decide to go to a Greek party with my friends. It was a nice girls-get-out-of-the-house night, which were few and far between. I usually spent my nights home when the Superstar went out with his friends (or wherever he actually went). But this night, I ran into none other but Mr. Constellation, standing with his friends. I attempted to walk past him with my drink, but he stopped me.

"Can I get a hug?" he said.

And I was thinking, *Hell no*, and looked at him with my "Are you serious?" face, but I still gave him a hug. I shouldn't have. That just gave him the opportunity he needed to know if the offer was still open.

I saw him around the club a couple times later while I enjoyed my time with my friends, dancing, laughing, drinking, and being silly, being the super-confident, unapproachable Shannon Dee. But later when I got home, I just so happened to get a text from Mr. Constellation, saying how interested he was in me even though he didn't want to come between me and my current boyfriend.

LESSON 12: SOME GUYS AREN'T MEANT FOR MORE THAN A CURSORY GLANCE.

Mr. Drama

He just wanted to use me for everything that he could get. He went from being sweet to being the most evil person I've ever met. At first he claimed he wanted to love me, but he really just wanted me to hate myself.

The Hip-Hop Head

The Hip-Hop Head is thoroughly intriguing. Not just his demeanor and style, cuz the boy can dress, but he is just downright *fine.* I can't even describe how majorly attractive he is. Truly a sight to see, and coming from me, that's a big deal. He's funny; it's cute. And he's different, really different. Kinda quirky, but not so much. Just cool as shit and laid back. He is himself. You can sense his confidence. It's just really very sexy, a very good look. Quite refreshing. But he's young. And that right there is the only turn-off. But still, I haven't been intrigued in a while. And I like different. Guys with their own swag are so attractive. Lol. Probably cuz they seem to be like me. I wanna get to know him better … I think we could be really cool. But … ehhhh, idk. I really don't think anyone deserves to know the complex yet simplistic person I am. And I hear he kinda gets around. But back to the Hip-Hop Head: He really is gonna make it somewhere in life cuz he's got beaucoup talent. And the sex appeal that exudes from his character can only help. He's really cool. But I believe that's as far as it will go. He's showed me it's okay to just admire and like someone and not take it too far. And I won't. But the thought that if I wanted to, I could, kinda makes me smile. If I wanted him, I could have him. But I think I'll just keep him as a friend.

Lesson 13: Some guys are better off as friends

The Artist

He was a great guy, a true gentleman, kind, caring, courteous, compassionate. A breath of fresh air. But I knew he wasn't for me. When we first met, he introduced me to his family and called me his fiancée.

The Fireman

He's a good guy. On his grown man mostly, working and taking care of business. But he's got baggage. Seems like too much for me: a son and a baby momma he used to live with. He wasn't right within, because he wouldn't face reality. He claims he enjoys my company; I think he's just looking for a rebound. He didn't marry his baby momma; why expect him to be serious?

Lesson 14: You'll never forget someone who changes your life.

Everyone and everything helps you grow in some way, but there are a few amazing people who really assist your growth; along with their help and God's, you can truly sprout and develop flawlessly.

God knows what you need. He will prepare you, give you knowledge and wisdom, prune you, and help you grow into his full potential for you. He is always on time.

The moral with dating is that you should never give a boyfriend husband privileges. Most guys just want to conquer a girl. I spent so long being second pick, being used, being abused; when someone wanted to make me first pick, I was scared. Someone who truly loves you, though, will help you work through all your pain. I was blessed to find my soulmate, the person I'd really been looking for all that time. I was always stumbling or falling in love. I finally learned how to stand in it, how to be strong and determined, how to follow my dreams and visions, how to be close to God. I started to be what I had the potential to be. I was so stifled in my relationships. I didn't set boundaries, which I needed. I couldn't focus on my dreams. I couldn't grow. I allowed myself, my time, my love, and my kindness to be manipulated. But in the end, these were just playmates, more or less: practice for the real thing. If I hadn't experienced the hurt or pain or trials and tribulations that I did with them, I never would have been prepared to experience these things and tougher circumstances as an adult.

Play with my mind, communicate with my spirit and soul. Pluck my heart strings, push me away, and let me grow.

My Superhero

When I first met him, we just clicked. I was modeling and following my purpose. I was growing mentally and working on myself physically. I was doing well. I was given such an amazing gift when God brought him into my life. Our first time meeting, he walked me to my car and kissed me on my forehead. The next time we met, he introduced me to his friends as his future wife: the manifestation of my dreams, and an embodiment of love. He brought color to my life, which had been gray. And over time, the colors steadily get brighter. He has the same mentality as me, but beyond. Reminds me so much of my first love. I totally admire him and how he stays on his grind. This in turn focuses me and allows me to follow my vision. Not a distraction, but gives a calmness and order to you. This is the type of guy I can respect enough to be with for real. He made me feel strong and courageous and like a true woman, but while being around him, I felt like a child. Being an alpha female, submission has always been an issue, but with him, it was natural. He's cool, sweet, understanding, and so much fun to be around. I am totally excited about someone finally. He turned out to be everything that I needed. It's hard being patient and waiting on Mr. Right, especially when Mr. Wrong and Mr. Right Now chase you, to no avail. But they say great takes time. You and that person have to be molded into the hundred you have to be to find one another. Being in love with him is so easy. Our relationship hasn't been easy; there have been ups and downs, times we spend apart. But I'm not scared that things won't work out. With him in my life, I've been strengthened. Everything is effortless, and that's how it should be.

It's interesting how much our relationship got hated on. That's how I knew how special it was. The enemies didn't want it to happen. Cuz with him, my life elevated. We helped each other through the ups and downs of life. That's what love really is about. We believed in each other and grew together. The right one will stay, while all the others fall away. Space, time, and loyalty are the best combinations for a winning relationship. He gave me everything I needed to become what I wanted to be and what I knew he needed. I am growing into an amazing woman, all in preparation for the future. And while I'm growing, he is also. It's amazing to witness the wonderful man he is becoming. I'm so proud of myself and of him. I'm thankful and so very grateful to God for allowing our lives to entwine. I no longer worry if we will end up together or who I will be with. I don't worry if he will find someone else or if things do not work between us. I just want him to be happy. I want him to grow. I feel selfless, as though it's no longer about me and what I want. I feel at peace with the process.

Even though I hoped for a happily ever after, I learned that your life is what you make it. I learned how to be myself and be comfortable with that, with just me alone. I learned how to stand on my own two feet. I learned how to be responsible for my own choices and decisions. I learned how to take adversity as it came and end up better from it. I learned how to view mistakes as learning experiences and nothing more. I could finally focus on myself, focus on my purpose. All because I no longer worried about finding someone to love me; I began to love myself. Not when I finally understood how much God loved me. I no longer sought validation from people. I no longer cared about what people said about me or how they felt about me.

I learned that what really mattered is what I said about me and how I felt about myself. I learned that I never needed anyone to save me; I needed to be introduced to the superhero within myself. I learned that I didn't need to be a woman who needed a man; I needed to become the woman a man needed. This was the best revelation that I could have received. I learned how to become the best version of myself from the love, strength, and courage our relationship gave me. And for that, I will always be grateful to him and everything else that led to our meeting. Now I understand the saying, "It is better to have loved and lost, than never to have loved at all." I can now say I truly know love. And as I let go and allow life to happen and allow him to grow into my life, I'm always ready for it. God taught me how to truly love by sending him into my life.

If ever there comes a day when I cannot tell you I love you, I pray that your heart remembers the feeling.

LESSON 15: YOUR RELATIONSHIPS SHOULD BEGIN WITH GOD.

For so long, I was doing relationships on my own. When I finally got to the relationship where I began to change, I began to wish that I had begun it as a godly relationship, instead of asking God to fix it in the end. I found myself regretting the years of spiritual absence, many sins, and many problems and mistakes. It took me a while to realize that I was in a good place, that I wanted to change, that I wanted to truly love another person as God had intended. This type of love is not easy and requires a lot of work, patience, and sacrifice. Focus on your purpose. Everything else will come along. John 4 tells the story of the woman at the well who God healed. She had had many husbands, and God told her that with him, she would never thirst again. God did amazing things in my life. He healed my soul. There is no possible way to thank him for his grace and mercy.

1. Place God first.

2. Stay focused.

3. Fruitfulness: If something isn't
good, don't keep it in your life.

4. Freedom: Don't let anyone hold you back.

5. Be fit for Christ.

6. Don't worry about what others may think of you.

7. God will make sure finances are fine.

8. Put your hand in God's hand.

LESSON 16: GOD WILL BRING YOU DOWN TO BRING YOU UP.

God does not change like man or anything else on the earth. He is always the same.

You have to struggle at some point. It is required in growth and learning. Nothing is easy. Or else you would not be better after experiencing it. In order to stand up, you have to know what it feels like to fall down.

When you go through hard times, you truly appreciate the good times later on. For so long, I couldn't understand why I had to go through such bad experiences. I thought, *I'm not as wrong as some people. I'm not hurting anyone. I'm a good person.* But for so long, I was hurting myself. Spiritually. I wasn't loving myself enough to not let others tear me down. With God, I became stronger.

LESSON 17: LIFE BEGINS WHERE FEAR ENDS.

Fear is a spirit not from God. There is nothing in life that you should fear.

After being hurt so many times, I was afraid of loving or showing my feelings to anyone. Being hurt and broken is how the enemy wants to keep you, which is why he presents temptations that look good to you, which he knows will hurt you. I thought for so long that sex and drugs would take the problem away. But it honestly only made the problems worse. I needed God in my life, and finding him was the best thing that ever happened to me. I stopped being afraid of everything in life. The enemy wants you to be afraid so he has power over you. Finding yourself and having a relationship with God is his worst nightmare.

In the Bible, it says that when you encounter many trials and testing of your faith, that is good because it produces endurance. Endurance is a great thing, as it makes you perfect and complete.

LESSON 18: I CAN BE CHANGED BY WHAT HAPPENS TO ME, BUT I REFUSE TO BE REDUCED BY IT.

Growth is change. It may look like the end of the world, because it is new, and you don't know what is going on or what will happen.

The pressure of growth changes you into something much more beautiful than you were.

In spite of any difficulties I have faced, I have gotten to experience some amazing things. I've gotten to model clothing for several designers, starting their brands in print and runway. I've gotten to travel to other countries, visit concentration camps, and experience things many people never have the opportunity to. I've been chosen to be in a major motion film. I've obtained my bachelor's degree, my master's degree, and several certificates as well. And I have experienced true love. God willing, I still have so much more to experience in life. And now I get to use the pain to help heal others.

We control the meaning we give to events in our life. Even though we often do not have control of the circumstances, we control what we think and how we feel about them. We either become a victim or become empowered. Victims look at things as though they were done to them and are hurt. Powerful people look at things as information and lessons, and when someone else comes along, they are stronger from them.

LESSON 19: WATCH THE COMPANY YOU KEEP.

True friends walk beside you, not in front of you or behind you. They treat you as an equal, support your happiness, and encourage your growth.

It has been said that when you are doing well, your friends know you, and when you are doing bad, you know your friends.

Throughout my life, I was often befriended by girls who admired me, only to become jealous of me and see me as competition. I say "girls: with pure meaning of the word: childish. A woman knows she has no competition. She is concerned with her purpose and appreciates other woman and their individuality. To be jealous of anyone shows that you have personal self-esteem issues and don't know your own worth.

The Faker: We were never friends in high school. I always suspected that she liked my boyfriend, even though my boyfriend and her boyfriend at the time were good friends. While in college, we came into contact again. At first, she was attempting to get me back with my ex-boyfriend. This slowly turned into the shocker that they were dating, and finally, they got married.

The Wicked Witches (Frenemies): They were drama. Always in my ear about drama. They wanted to be me, which was sad. They didn't love themselves, so they didn't want me to love myself either or to be with anyone who loved me. They had both been hurt, but instead of healing themselves, like I did, they were just bitter. They were disloyal and wanted to be single forever, be sinful, and use people. And even though I didn't believe in what they did, I wanted to be a friend and not judge them, til I realized that birds of a feather flock together, and I wasn't a bird. I had to leave them behind. It became clear that they didn't want what was best for me. As my life started to progress, they seemed angry with the things I became blessed with.

To get anywhere on your journey, you must learn to walk alone.

I was so focused on people and worldly things and their ideas. And that is not where your focus should be. Oftentimes, my friends were simply enablers; they had the same bad habits I did (or their habits were a bit worse, to where I didn't feel left out).

The Bible says that bad company corrupts good character. So if those around you are doing things that are not good, you must learn to walk alone. Following the crowd is not always good, especially if they are not going where you want to be.

LESSON 20: NOT EVERYONE HAS YOUR BEST INTEREST AT HEART.

People say you've changed when you stop being the person they want you to be, when you stop being like they want you to be or how they expect you to be.

Sex is not a game. Playing with hearts is not a game. For so long, I let my exes play with my heart and mind in hopes that they would love me.

People you believe are there for you are not always there for you. Many times, I've experienced people who are in my life for them. They attempt to gain from who they associate with.

LESSON 21: YOU CAN'T MAKE SOMEONE LOVE YOU.

I was looking for love in all the wrong places. Every time I didn't find it, I'd feel even more empty and broken. I would believe that this time, things would work. This time, he'll love me and not just the things I do for him.

Love, love, love, love, love

So I was just thinking, when you love someone, and I mean truly love them, all you want is to get along with them; I'm totally thinkin' 'bout my favorite old Kelis song, "Get Along with You"; the song emphasizes how someone's love and the need to get along with them is more substantial than material possessions and even the world itself (taken straight from Wikipedia). By "get along," I mean understand them, you know, mesh well. Now if you love this person, you know you can't change them and wouldn't wanna anyways, cuz you still love the things about them that drive you crazy. But what can be done to help the process? Being understanding, puttin' in the effort to learn how they are, how they act, and how you should react to it to produce a favorable outcome. Yeah, it's a lot of work to truly get to know someone, but with love, everything is possible. Love makes all that hard work seem easy and so worth the time.

We've all been to school; to understand a subject and prosper with that knowledge, you have to learn it. That takes time and effort. Do you think it would take anything less to learn about a person? We are just as complex as books. :) Just think of your love as some sort of higher education.

What? I'm a romantic! Lol!

Be an asset, not a liability.

LESSON 22: WHEN PEOPLE SHOW YOU WHO THEY ARE, BELIEVE THEM.

Values, morals, integrity, and character should be your main focus when befriending anyone. You should befriend those who hold you accountable.

Lately, I've been thinkin' about life and people and analyzing things a lot. I am nowhere near perfect; I will put that out there. I do not claim to know everything, cuz honestly, I really don't claim to be all that smart. I totally believe Socrates' theory that the man who knows something knows that he knows nothing at all. But I am very confused as to why people do the things they do, especially in this case. I know people in their own way are selfish. With that said, I will ask, how can you ever be with someone the way God meant men and women to be? If both people are worried 100 percent about what they want, which is wanting their cake and eating it too, how will they ever have 50/50 to put into a relationship, to be able to commit to someone? I wonder when people change from bein' players and all that to bein' faithful to just one person. I always wondered how this happens. But now I realize that when people take the time out of their lives (this is where being selfless and humbling themselves begins) to ponder how they are and how they act and why they do, when they take the time out to analyze themselves and reflect on their lives and relationships, that is when they begin seeing God's plan. That is when they grow and become a true adult. When they realize, "Wow, everything really is not about just me in my life." If you think about it, older generations look at our generation on this subject and usually shake their heads. I mean, most younger people in their twenties have slept around with more people (I think it's multiplied by about three or more) than older people have slept with in their lives. That is so sad to me. But that process takes a level of maturity. What level are you on? Most of y'all are not on mine. Ponder that, people.

I thought about writing today but I felt u don't deserve it,

2 know how I feel n what's in my heart n know how badly u've hurt it.

On one side I think, *Man things would be so great if* ... but then I realize that "if" will never b.

I can no longer b concerned with u or what I hoped 4 us; I gotta b concerned with me. Love love love love love ... in fact, it is such a simple thing.

Adoration, respect, trust, honesty, selflessness, all the feelings n emotions that make ur heart sing, but I question, is it there, like is it truly there, can u see, cuz I don't think it's in ur heart but just what I'm wanting n hoping for me. Am I blinding myself with what I'm wishing 4?

I don't know n really don't wanna find out cuz that answer would probably hurt me exponentially, hurt me even more.

I don't wanna know.

I've been contemplating everything so much lately, and I've been thinkin' so much ... and then I wonder, Why do I think so much? Why aren't my friends goin' through the same things I am? And if you really knew me, you know I talk a lot and ask a lot of questions that most of you can't answer. Especially lately, but that's just my way of ... I dunno ... experiencing. Maybe this is just my time to mature. I know everything happens for a reason and God has a plan for everyone; maybe now is just my time to actually realize that. My life has been the best and worst story ever, better than any movie I've ever seen or book I've ever read. It's had ups and downs, sad times, funny times, hilarious times, very painful times, everything that can be imagined. But I'm kinda proud cuz I don't think many people could have made it through. There's no one I know who is exactly like me, who acts exactly the same and has been through the exact same things. I'm one of a kind, a rare breed. And at the end of the day, that point right there makes me happy and quite optimistic. Man, I love my life and everyone and everything that has been a part of this journey. Bad or good, it still has shaped me and made me the complex/intricate yet simplistic person that I am. I learn so much from you all, and I know you prolly don't realize it, but I truly do. And I'm more than grateful, really. Thanks!

In this day and age, you can find out anything about anyone on Facebook. You all know this. I find out so much stuff I don't even wanna know, cuz I'm nosey as all hell, I'm analytical, and most of all, I think it's funny as shit when people lie. I don't lie, so I find the opposite in thought intriguing. I correct people's words. I used to point out when my teachers made a mistake; I correct people's spelling, grammar, use of context, and I was just the smart ass who was just bein' real all my life. Lol. I like to keep people on their toes and expect the same for me from them. Proving people wrong when they're lying is cool as shit to me; what's done in the dark always comes to light. I love when people underestimate me and insult my intelligence. Gives me somethin' to do. Lol. Don't get me wrong, it usually pisses me off, but I have like a twenty-second rebound rate, and I'm back to bein' the conniving li'l people-watcher who loves the world. Lol. (Totally in an innocent, curious way, lol.) But I am usually the one who will say things everyone else thinks but doesn't say, only cuz I could care less how I'm thought about for saying it (even though I do sporadically say things to my friends on this subject). If you gotta problem, square up; mentally, I'll break you down before you can try and fight me (I don't fight, I beat bitches' asses), but I'm too cute to fight (and grown and sexy, I might add). I am a New Yorker, meaning I am cocky as shit, but I grew up in the South, which is where I learned how to be hospitable. I dub myself the candy-coated peach. (Get it? New York's fruit is the apple, and Georgia's is the peach; I'm a genius, I know, and I love candy apples, so if you

ever get me one, I'll love you for life. Lol, literally.)
Yeah, I know, toot toot on my own horn. But just
basically, I am grown, okay? Remember that. But I
digress; here's my point: I absolutely hate when chicks
add me on their Facebook to try and find out who I
am. Fuck! How many licks does it take to get to the
center of a Tootsie Pop? The world may never know.
Remember that commercial? That's how I feel about
your questioning who I am. The world may never
know; just respect that shit. I especially get pissed
when they've found my page from a guy's. Nope, I'm
not a hoe, nor do I want your man (if he wants me, I
can't help that; not my concern). I am just a cool ass,
down ass chick that some people admire, and some do
hate me too. But shit, they hate me cuz they're haters;
that's their job. Usually I will ask who the person
is; I personally send a "Do I know you?" message.
Most of the time, the question is totally rhetorical,
cuz I know who you are but am tryin' to feel you
out as a person. Hmmm, ponder that. But this keeps
happening, so now I gotta talk it out. I'm not sayin'
this about everyone. Don't read it and be offended.
But if you are, I'd love to hear about it. :) Stop bein'
so damn insecure. But if you are, be real about the
shit. "Hey, Shannon, I am so-and-so, and the reason
I added you is cuz I saw you on so-and-so's page and
wanted to figure out who you were to them." I totally
respect honesty and realness and will reply with a
real-as-hell answer; you'd be surprised. I mean, shit,
I've had insecurities in life of my own. Who cares?

Own that shit! I don't like drama. I don't start shit at all, but if you bring it or disrespect me in any way, I will have to tear you to shreds; usually not literally, but pride does go a long way when someone hurts it. I have no problem whatsoever knockin' people off their high horse. (I might be a li'l immature in that thought, but oh well.) That's if I'm even interested in it enough. I'm pretty nonchalant sometimes. Lol. Anyhow, just don't try no fuckin' shit, okay? Okay?

LESSON 23: NEVER THINK SOMEONE WOULD DO FOR YOU WHAT YOU'D DO FOR THEM.

You should always treat people how you want to be treated, despite how they actually treat you. Your actions reflect your character, while their actions reflect theirs.

Okay, okay, aiight, aiight. I'm 'bout to get on my soap box for just a minute, and I ain't gonna stay on it long, cuz personally, I think teachin' is a profession that comes wit monetary compensation …

I will define these two words for y'all, cuz some people don't seem to know what they mean.

Loyalty: as a general term, this signifies a person's devotion or sentiment of attachment to a particular object, which may be another person or group of persons, an ideal, a duty, or a cause. It expresses itself in both thought and action and strives for the identification of the interests of the loyal person with those of the object.

Real: authentic, genuine, not pretended, sincere.

I read people quite easily, and that is exactly why I don't like too many people. But I respect people for what they are, so basically, I can take a person at face value. You are what you are; who am I to judge? I'm not a hater; I believe that is distasteful. I'm not fake, quite distasteful also. But snitchin'? That will get you killed; good thing I'm not really into murderin' folks.

But with that bein' said, it's hard to get my respect. Now if you have it, that is me acknowledgin' I think you might be kinda real, like I am. Now if you had it and you lost it, that's no bueno.

I tend to forget everyone isn't like me. I tend to forget that some people just aren't all that real. I tend to forget that you can only trust someone as far as you can throw them.

So let's recap:

"Hear no evil, see no evil, speak no evil." I don't know shit.

I will say the same thing in front of one person that I will say in front of anyone. I don't just claim to be neutral, I actually am neutral.

But hey, I'm quite nonchalant, and I really could care less how other people live their life.

Like I said, who am I to judge?

This is chess, people; grow up.

Fight for You

I love u so much that I will fight 4 u.

I'd even go so far 2 the extent of fighting u, 4 u.

Fighting ur pride n ego, insecurities, doubts, fears …

sad times, bad times, regrets, pains n tears.

Love is not always easy, there's
plenty bads n goods …
hard times, tough times, it's GONNA
rain, that's 2 b understood.   But I, the
one who loves u forever n a day,
will always be here …

fighting 4 u …

til I can make u stay.

LESSON 24: LOVE TIMING ISSUE.

This advice I received from a male friend may be the best advice I was ever given.

He told me I need to let a boy focus until he grows into the man he is meant to be. He told me I have to let a man get to a place where he is not just thinking of his right now, but of his future. Basically, he must grow in himself. A man needs to prove to a woman and to himself that he can provide and take care of himself and one day her and the family. He said I must not resist change but must be patient and go with the flow of life. There is no one outside of someone that can change someone or make them grow. They must do it for themselves.

LESSON 25: DON'T LET YOUR TRIALS MAKE YOU BITTER.

Your life must be lived with no regrets. Our scars make us who we are.

There's a saying that you can grow bitter or get better; the choice is yours. Through the trials and tribulations you encounter, you can grow and become stronger, or shrink and let them weaken you.

LESSON 26: CHANGE YOUR THOUGHTS, CHANGE YOUR LIFE.

You are a total product of your thoughts. Your mind is so powerful that you become what you think.

If you think you can do something, then you can, and if you think you cannot do something, then once again, you will be correct.

To stop being a slave to others and even your own self, you must free yourself from mental slavery.

To be free in your mind is true freedom. If your mind is not free, you are not free. To be alive and not be free in your mind is not better than being dead, because mentally, you really are not living. Proof of true existence comes from having a free mind.

Your thoughts lead to purpose, which leads to action. This leads to habits, which lead to character. Character is the only thing that can fix your destiny.

Your standards should be that of God's. He is the bar. He gives us intuition to use. Once I started believing and trusting in God, my whole life changed. I always had a problem trusting people. I let this worldly idea transfer over to my faith. You must truly believe, with no other option, in the word of God.

When your mind is renewed by experience and wisdom, you are transformed into the best version of yourself. The Bible says you will then be able to discern God's will and what is good, acceptable, and perfect.

Lesson 27: Obedience.

Give God your worries. Give him your problems. Give him the broken parts of you. He will fix you. I was so stuck with trying to help myself. I used drugs, sex, and alcohol to dull the pain I felt from heartbreak and disappointment but that never worked. I came to a point in my life where I'm like, "God, I trust you. If you can make this pain inside go away, please just do it." But then I had to follow his lead and no longer attempt to lead on my own.

You should never become weary in doing good, the Bible says. You must work to plant the seeds as well as work to harvest. If you do not give up, you will gain a reward.

Lesson 28: Be patient.

When you believe in God and trust him, there is honestly nothing you should be anxious for. Whether you see it or not, he is working things out on your behalf all the time. There is a process you must go through to become who you are meant to be. As a seed grows, so must a person. As fruit ripens, so must a person. You learn so much from nature, including the importance of timing and patience. I didn't understand this until I grew more mature. And as I continue to mature, I have a much greater understanding that everything happens in due time. Life is to be lived and never rushed. God's timing is better than any timing you could have hoped for.

There is never anything you should be anxious about. You should pray and work and allow God to then do his part. He loves you and wants the best for you and will give you everything you need when the time is right.

LESSON 29: NOTHING WORTH HAVING COMES EASILY.

You must follow your purpose. God doesn't make mistakes. He gave me creativity. You must walk in faith. There is always an element of uncertainty and the unknown. Faith that can't be tested, can't be trusted. You must step past ongoing distractions and doubts. Storms come not to harm you but to prepare and strengthen you. We have to push through; pain is part of our process.

You must be strong and endure greatly to receive what is meant for you. Even though what is meant for you is for you and you alone, you must have enough strength to obtain it.

LESSON 30: GIVE PEOPLE TIME TO SHOW THEIR TRUE COLORS.

People of good character are kind to others. They are nice to those who cannot do them any good, as well as those who cannot fight back. It is very important to see how others treat these two types of people. It will tell you much about the kind of person they are.

I'm the type of person who always wants to believe that there is some good inside of everyone. I know this isn't always true. Some people have no good inside of them. I tend to give people the benefit of the doubt. I guess that's my burden: being a good person. I like to believe that everyone can be good.

Risks

I ain't wrote in a minute, but it's ALWAYS there,
the thoughts in my mind make up the atmosphere,
and right now everything around me is a whirlwind
I do, I don't, I want to, but I can't let you in …

cuz this ain't what I planned for,
but I doubt you did either,
tryna take it oh so s-l-o-w, but still seeming eager
but … I don't know how to change that, I wish I did
grown as hell, but got me feelin' like a kid … cuz …

I HAVE SUCH A CRUSH ON YOU …

but I play it cool, or at least I try to …
In between my ears, you're kinda gettin' in it.
Hold up, gotta slow down, gotta take a minute …
to assess the damage of what could happen; this
road ain't paved, it's crazy, and I need a map and …

I CAN'T GO THERE AGAIN …

Pump the breaks!
But wait, I'm already there … I'm already too late.

I'm just hoping it's really okay to take risks …

LESSON 31: GROWTH.

I haven't written in a while. As my loyal note readers know, I thoroughly believe that teaching should come with monetary compensation. Lol! And it will, when I finish my book. :-D But in this case, I'm going to be a blessing, to whoever needs to read this. This world is cold. It truly truly is a cold, cold world. But you should not wish it were easier, you should wish you were better. And guess what? You can be! All you have to do is work on it. Sounds easy, but the work is in the doing, in your actions. Everyone was given a light. "This little light of mine, I'm gonna let it shine," and to let it shine, you have to control what gets to it. If any ol' gust of wind can put out your fire, how will you survive? In the real world, a light wind is not the only thing coming for your light. Trust me! The things that come to put it out get stronger. Therefore, to control what gets to it, you must be stronger. Your skin must be as strong as armor. You must love yourself enough to strengthen your skin and your light. Strengthen your heart. You must work on you, becoming the best you that you can be. How you do that is personal. There are many ways, and it's different for everyone. No one walks the same path or takes the same journey.

The best advice I can give is, get used to being alone. Being alone is not a bad thing. As I stated, no one walks the same path. Not at first, anyways, but that's for "Only the strong survive" lesson, and I personally haven't completed all of that yet. Lol! I digress. Work on you, bettering yourself. Don't worry about everyone else. Love yourself, love your family, love those who treat you right. Be humble, and be grateful for everything, because everything happens for a reason. Life is about learning. He won't put more on you than you can handle. You have to trust yourself and wish you were better, not that things were easier.

Good luck! :-D

Lesson 32: Happiness is an inside job.

For so long, I depended on others to make me happy. And when they didn't, I'd feel the pain of disappointment. For so long, I was attempting to give my heart to someone instead of giving it to God first. My priorities were off. I had good intentions, but they weren't right. When I started to depend on myself for my happiness and the God that lives within me, I stopped feeling that way. I began to feel fulfilled without the interference of my old worldly lifestyle. When I began to see life as something I didn't deserve and something that was given as a gift, my idea of happiness changed. I began to truly know the feeling of joy. The only thing that can truly fill you up is a relationship with God.

Faith and trust in God gives so much peace. The most important thing I have found is to have peace of mind.

Lesson 33: You are responsible for your own success.

It has been said that to know others is intelligence, while knowing yourself is true wisdom; to master others is strength, while mastering yourself is true power. It is not enough to know and understand the outside, you must subsequently know and understand the inside.

Get to know God. That is where success comes from. Serve God, not man.

You must believe you will receive what you are working for. You have to see it and have faith in it before it will be given to you. Once you figure out what in fact it is you want in your life, you have a better chance of attracting it.

Law of Attraction

You attract what you put out. If you're putting yourself out there with no clothes, and your body is what you are showing off, your body will be the only thing a man wants, especially when you are young, and they have no interest in pursuing a relationship with you. Relationships are a sign of maturity. If you are not mature in the first place, how can you expect a long-lasting relationship? Yes, the fairytale that is put in girls' heads of having a prince come marry them is sweet, but it's not fully true. And with the influence of sex added on top of that view, you assume that just because a man has sex with you that he will want more than that. That is the worst assumption one could make.

Self-Reflection, Evolve

I didn't understand what real, true love was. There is no possible way you can understand it at a young age. We are imperfect beings, trying to possess a perfect virtue. We can only do that when we ourselves have become as close to perfect as we can. We can only do that once we find ourselves and become the spiritual beings we were created to be. To become a spiritual being, you must first become whole. You have to work on yourself and fill yourself before you can fill others. As a young girl, I thought love meant that I needed someone to complete me. At that age, it was more like 50 plus 50 equaling 1. That is not what is needed. A complete being with their 100 and another complete being with their 100 combine to complement one another. Yin to a yang. You have to love yourself. If you don't love yourself, someone will come along and teach you how to hate yourself. Love is a learned emotion. If you never learn something, how can you teach it to someone else?

"Remove those 'I want you to like me' stickers from your forehead and, instead, place them where they truly will do the most good: on your mirror" (Susan Jeffers). No fear! Fake fear is an obstacle that can paralyze you if you let it. It is the absence of faith. The only thing that should be feared is God.

Failure is not an option.

Learn to let go. Stop holding on to the past: people, situations, circumstances. Change is the only constant in life.

If you do what you've always done, you'll get what you've always gotten.

A very important part of working on yourself is making your weaknesses your strengths as well. There is only a weakness because you are not as good at it as other things. But if you make that a strength as well, then there is nothing you cannot do.

LESSON 34: GET RID OF YOUR COMFORT ZONE.

If your hands are not free and open, you are not in a place to be given more.

Being uncomfortable isn't all that great of a feeling. It wasn't a great feeling for me at first. The idea of change and the unknown used to scare me. But you can't grow when you're comfortable. And if you're holding onto something so tightly in your clenched fist, there is no room for anything else to come into your hand. My comfort zone had a lot to do with relationships, friendships, material things, job security, ideas, even where I lived.

Lesson 35: Live life with the mind-set of a contender.

You're never too old to learn. People should be like sponges, soaking up information while on their journey. You never know who will be your teacher. Be hungry but never be thirsty. Always work to be better.

Lesson 36: Don't place values on the opinions of others over God.

Sometimes, you have to do what is best for yourself, no matter what anyone else thinks. It's been said that other people are our worst enemy when it comes to destroying our instincts. Some people are H.A.T.E.R.S.: Having Animosity Toward Everyone Reaching Success. In life, there will always be people who are "testing" you, attempting to see how much they can push you or how much they can take from you. Once you know yourself and your personal truths, these attempts no longer become issues. Some people have good advice toward your journey, but God is the only one you need to verify with.

I never claim to be perfect. I don't claim to be better than anyone, but I know I am better than I was yesterday, and I am so ready to be better and better and better.

There have been plenty of times where people didn't believe in me: strangers, my friends, even my family. There have even been plenty of times where I would start to not believe in myself. But true strength, courage, and determination will get you through anything. You must believe in yourself. Some people react strongly to criticism and judgment. Many have committed suicide due to the issue. If you are doing what you know is right and what God has set as the purpose in your life, take opinions of others with a grain of salt, as the saying goes. Everyone has their opinion. Everyone has their personal experiences. You just have to take with you what is best for you and leave the rest. If I had listened to people and their diagnoses, I would have believed I was crazy, psychotic, and depressed.

The plan that God has for you is so much better than any plan you could have for yourself.

LESSON 37: PERFECT YOUR CHARACTER.

A virtue is a good habit that enables us to act according to right reason, enlightened by faith. I learned what are considered good virtues for a person. I found that faith, according to Hebrews 11:1, is "the assurance of things hoped for, the conviction of things not seen." Hebrews 10:23 mentions hope: "Let us hold fast the confession of our hope without wavering, for He who promised is faithful." I learned that hope is our trust in Christ's promises.

I studied the virtue of charity and learned that it is to treat our neighbor as our brother. I learned how important it is to be generous and self-sacrificing. I learned that in Christian theology, charity (or love) is the greatest of the three theological virtues.

Love, in this sense of an unlimited loving-kindness toward all others, is held to be the ultimate perfection of the human spirit, because it is said to both glorify and reflect the nature of God. In its most extreme form, such love can be self-sacrificial. Confusion can arise from the multiple meanings of the English word "love." Love is distinguished by its origin, being divinely infused into the soul, and by its residing in the will rather than emotions, regardless of what emotions it stirs up. This love is necessary for salvation, and with it, no one can be lost. I learned that prudence is correct knowledge of things to be done or avoided. I learned that justice is our constant and permanent determination to give everyone their rightful due. I learned about temperance, which is the virtue that moderates the desire for pleasure. I learned how important constraint was. I learned that a constant mindfulness of others and one's surroundings, and practicing self-control, abstention, moderation, and deferred gratification, were perfect ways to live a great life.

I learned that the virtue of fortitude, or courage, is firmness of spirit and steadiness of will in doing good, despite obstacles in the performance of our daily duty. I learned about chastity, which is abstaining from sexual conduct, and that the practice of courtly love and romantic friendship is the true way a relationship should begin. I learned the importance of cleanliness through cultivating good health and hygiene, and to maintain it by refraining from intoxicants. I learned to be honest with oneself, one's family, one's friends, and to all of humanity. I learned to embrace the idea of moral wholesomeness and achieving purity of thought through education and betterment. I studied how to refrain from being distracted or influenced by hostility, temptation, or corruption. I learned to be diligent and serious as well as careful about my nature in my actions and work. I learned to have a decisive work ethic. I learned to be steadfast in my beliefs and not let anyone sway me.

Your intuition is very strong. Within yourself, you really know what is true. I learned about fortitude and not giving up. I learned how to budget my time by monitoring my own activities to guard against laziness. I learned to uphold my convictions at all times, especially when no one else is watching. I learned the importance of integrity. I learned how to be patient and accept forbearance and endurance through moderation. I learned to resolve conflicts and injustice peacefully, as opposed to resorting to violence. I learned how to forgive and to show mercy to sinners.

I learned how important it is to not kill or be violent in any way to any life form or sentient being. I studied about practicing moderation of meat consumption and being healthy and eating better food. I learned the importance of being peaceful and kind. I learned to be empathetic and give unconditional love and voluntary kindness, just to give it. I learned the importance of having a positive outlook and cheerful demeanor as well as what an amazing thing it is to inspire kindness in others. I learned humility and to be modest in my behavior. I learned to be selfless and to give respect to all who cross my path. I learned how courageous someone is to undertake difficult tasks and graciously accept the sacrifices involved. I learned to revere those who have wisdom and selflessly teach in love. I learned to give credit where it is due and not glorify my own self. I learned to be faithful to promises, as my word is all I have. I learned to not despair but trust God through it all and to not confront fear, uncertainty, or intimidation but let them pass.

When you want your own way and don't do what you're supposed to, you miss out on your blessings. One day when I was younger, my parents were taking my brother and me to visit my aunts, my dad's sisters. My mom told us to be in the house at a certain time to get ready to go. We lost track of time and were late coming in. My parents were a little upset, but they still took us. But what we didn't know until we got there was that my aunt had a pool. My father hadn't told us to bring our swimming stuff because we hadn't listened. My soulmate believes in this type of "tough love," just like my father. It's kind of funny, cuz they both are Leos.

But even more, God believes in this type of love. He loves you, despite any wrongs you have done. Yet this does not mean he is not upset by your wrongdoings or that they do not have consequences.

LESSON 38: FORGIVENESS IS KEY.

It is important to forgive others, but it is most important to forgive yourself. Sometimes, you have to tell yourself you did the best you could with where you were at that point in time. A key concept is "If you knew better, you'd do better." In hindsight, there are so many things I could have done differently, things I could have done right or done better. But with knowing that, I know how much I've grown. In life, you make mistakes, but as long as you learn from them and don't repeat them, you are moving forward. Even if you do repeat them a few times, keep trying, and eventually you will learn from them. This has been a large issue in my life. I was so ashamed by some of the events of my past that I couldn't accept being forgiven. I couldn't believe that God would forgive me, and ultimately, it was because I couldn't forgive myself. I've felt guilty about some things in my past for years. Then I realized that I finally had to just let it go. Your past and all those lessons you learn prepare you for your future.

I used to be so hurt by things others would say or do to me. That in turn would have me be harder on myself than I needed to be. Situations and experiences would make me feel guilty. I had to learn to forgive people and things and myself. When I learned this, I became a better person. I no longer took things personally.

LESSON 39: YOU'RE A PRICELESS BEING.

Within you is the power to create, the power to nurture, and the power to transform. Do you know how *amazing* you truly are?

You must know your worth. You must make yourself a marketable product. You must add value to yourself. Know your abilities.

Role Models/The Industry/ Sex Sells

Sex is not a bad thing. God created sex, but man perverted it. Fornication is what is bad. As far as role models, young girls don't seem to have any nowadays.

Their idea of a model is a video vixen or someone they see on TV. They believe that being naked will get them the attention they want. Such beautiful girls, selling their soul for attention. Our generation is the generation of entertainment, technology, and music videos. I love music too; I work in the entertainment industry, but it is not for everyone. A model gets paid to have her picture taken and promote a product. It is a job, an art form. It is hard work. The video vixen is closer to porn than the art of modeling. They are degraded to keep them weak, because a woman has power beyond measure. The perfect cookie-cutter image is what we are sold. That makes us feel bad about our imperfections. No one is perfect. And what is seen on TV is usually just an image. I want to show the world that imperfections are acceptable. Even with problems, you can still be whatever it is that you dream of being. I hear many people give excuses of why they can't do something: I'm not this, or I'm not that, I don't have this, or I don't have that. I'm not pretty enough, smart enough, blah blah blah. I want to challenge that. If I could do it, so can you. When you believe in yourself, anything is possible. Get rid of negative thoughts.

God gives an amazing image of what a woman should be. It is Proverbs 31 in the Bible. Read it and remember it. Emulate the wife of noble character and apply these teachings to your life.

I am a woman, the woman my parents raised me to be. Tough as nails, but I also have my soft side. I am independent and headstrong. Yet I am generous, caring, and sentimental. I possess all the superwoman powers of my mother. I can cook, clean, and take care of myself, and I could easily take care of someone else, just to name a few things. From my father, I can change my oil, change my tires, fix my brakes: the usual guy stuff. I possess the strength to get me where I need to be, no matter what. I have morals, values, my own mind, and my own opinions. I am blunt, and I am real; my father taught me life isn't sugarcoated. I am a strong black woman, what they raised me to be, at the tender age of twenty-four. I don't need someone to take care of me or make me strong or mold me into a woman; I am already there. What I need is someone to be there for me and have my back at times I don't feel so strong. I am a woman who does not need to be completed. I am not a clueless young girl. I am a woman who only needs completion. I can do for myself, but it'd be nice to know in my mind I don't always have to. It would be nice to have someone there. But most guys are not ready for that yet. I am only ready cuz I was taught well and prepared. Many people weren't. I've dealt with heartache because of this, because who I love is not ready for what could be, what I am. But it's better to have loved and lost than never to have loved at all, right? And if you let something go and it comes back, then it was truly meant to be. I will wait on my real, hoping he comes sooner than later, and I am okay with that. There is no settling. Others might be sad at this realization and ask, "So why was I made to be this strong black woman?" But I know I was created this way because that is what a real woman should be.

LESSON 40: FREEDOM.

To be free is to have options, options to do what you love, pursue happiness, and get the most out of life.

Shine your light. You must go forward. And while you are steadily progressing on your journey, refuse to turn back. Don't look back, don't look down, don't look left or right, look forward or look up. Look at your goals and your vision.

LESSON 41: LOVE CONQUERS ALL.

I learned what a soulmate was. I learned they are someone who has locks that fit our keys and keys that fit our locks. They make us feel safe enough to open the locks and let our true self step out. Then we can be who we truly are, completely, honestly, and authentically. We can be loved for our real self. Our soul mate makes life come to life.

Experiencing love from a true friend, from God, as well as abundantly from myself, I grew tremendously. That story from my past is no longer my story. I now have a different story to tell. Most of my experiences, I no longer remember. They no longer resonate with the person I have become. I am a conqueror, and I conquered my past in preparation for the bright future ahead that God has planned for me.

LESSON 42: LET GO AND LET GOD.

As humans, we feel the need to control that which we honestly have no control over. We must have enough faith in God and let him worry about those things. He already knows everything we're worrying about and everything that's going on in our life. God wants people to surrender to his will and honor him, the one who created us. He knows us better than we know ourselves. He also knows the plans he has for us.

LESSON 43: BROKEN PIECES CAN BE PUT BACK TOGETHER WHEN THEY ARE HEALED.

I want to leave you with the meaning of true love.

Everyone else was just a preview and practice in preparation of the real thing. It is said that you must experience bad before you experience good, or you will not be able to appreciate it. You must experience darkness before light.

I was so hurt by all the pain of being heartbroken that I let it add up. I never realized in relationships that everyone is going to hurt you at some point in time. You just have to find the ones who are worth suffering for. Never give up; you can make it through anything. God gives us adversity to shape us and make us better.

LESSON 44: DON'T TAKE THINGS PERSONALLY.

Never let the ignorance of others affect you.

People are imperfect beings. You must learn to love them regardless of their actions.

When there was a perfect being on this earth, we crucified him. After I became successful, I'm not sure if it was the God inside of me or my actual success that caused people to start treating me strangely. Friends and even family began to treat me badly. The more I attempted to get my life together, to be the best me that I could be, and to tend to my career, the more it seemed they didn't like it. I've heard the saying before that you can be successful, just don't be too successful, and don't be more successful than those around you. I didn't understand it at first. Now

I do. Nobody wants you to outgrow them. Nobody likes someone who's taller than them. They secretly are jealous. But jealousy is just the art of counting someone else's blessings. Many people look at the blessings of others and compare them with their own. This should never be an issue. Everyone is blessed and special in their own way. When you are grateful and thankful for everything you have (and do not have), you figure out there is no point in worrying about others. After a while, I stopped caring altogether about the opinions of people. I would say the best thing to do is take the good with the bad, but sometimes it's not. Sometimes, you must set up your own force field to not let the negative affect you.

LESSON 45: BALANCE.

Balance is the most important aspect of life. Balance in work and play. Time. Love. You must learn to love yourself enough to have balance in all areas. To do good in one area and not be doing well in another is not all the way good. To be great, you must be doing well across the board.

LESSON 46: ACQUIRE WISDOM AND GAIN KNOWLEDGE.

Only God knows his plan for your life. All you can do is be the best version of yourself to receive the blessings he has for you. Every day, you should be learning and growing as you go along on your journey. If you ask for wisdom, you will receive it.

LESSON 47: YOU ATTRACT WHAT AND WHO YOU NEED TO TAKE YOU TO THE NEXT LEVEL.

The worst thing you can do for someone is something they should be doing for themselves. Because you are in all actuality stunting their growth, forcing them to grow, when they should grow on their own. Most often, this can harm someone more than it can help them. Surround yourself with people and things that help you grow.

LESSON 48: LIVE A LIFE OF SERVICE.

This is how you truly make a difference in the world, by doing God's will. Be selfless. Help people, and they will in turn help you.

LESSON 49: SELF-ESTEEM IS NOT THE SAME AS PRIDE.

A humble person is someone who does not boast or try to impress. Don't just admire others and look down at yourself. Being humble doesn't mean you can't feel good about yourself. You must be confident, yet you must still have humility.

For so long, I admired others and their strength and how they overcame hardships and obstacles. After writing my book, I look back and am amazed that I too am an overcomer. I couldn't have made it to where I am without God and his grace. He is what you see when you look at me now, not the person I used to be.

LESSON 50: I JUST WANT TO BE YOUR INSPIRATION.

Learn from those you admire, and use what they have taught you. You recognize what you see in them, because it is in you as well. Remember that what God has for you, is for you and you alone.

Don't be like me, be better than me.

My goal is to motivate, inspire, and help enlighten others. I'm an overcomer, and you can be too!

I've fallen short so many times and disappointed God in so many ways, and still he loves me. I am his masterpiece. He loves me unconditionally and is proud of me and forgives me for all my mistakes. When I shook off the guilt and condemnation, I could still be what God intended me to be. God didn't give up on me. If I could make it, anybody can.

Find what you love to do, what you are passionate about, and learn how to make money doing it. Make that into your career.

LESSON 51: TRAGEDY.

The person I was so in love with, my Superhero, my twin flame, my true soulmate, was killed. It took me years to heal from this. I fell very low after this experience. I would cry, I was so hurt and upset and angry. I felt out of control. I almost went back to the rehab center, as I felt as though I could not control myself. I got to a place where I was mad at God and wondered why he would give me such a gift and take it away. He taught me about love. I knew love because of him; how could God take him away? I forgot everything I learned, or so I thought. (Later I found out these things were ingrained and instilled in me and couldn't be forgotten.) I questioned myself; what did I know? I questioned God for years. How could he hurt me so? I found out about all the Superhero's skeletons. I was not the only one. It hurt for a very long time. It took me a long time to come to the realization that my Superhero had taught me what I needed to know, but he wasn't perfect; he was human as well. No one would be able to replace him, but I realized no one would have to. His presence in my life was perfect, and for that, he will always be truly loved. God will not take something away from you without giving you something better. A seed is planted beneath the soil before it grows. It must push up through the ground until it reaches the light, and even then it grows higher. A young seedling is vulnerable and easy to be trampled, not as hard as a seed before it sprouts. Still it must do what it is meant to do: grow until it is stronger.

LESSON 52: YOU NEVER KNOW.

In the three years since Lesson 50, I have learned so much. I have taken steps forward and taken steps back. I have gone down to the lowest of the lows, but I have bounced back. As I have said, a seed is buried deep down in the dirt before it comes up and breaks through the ground to get to the sunlight. I have successfully manifested everything on my vision boards for the past four years. I have dated and had relationships and friendships. I have completed my schooling, ending up with several degrees and certifications. I have made a career for myself and am living on my own and taking care of my own responsibilities. I am serving others and helping them to grow and live their dreams.

I was recently taken off my bipolar medication and have been doing very well. The doctors had said the disease is incurable and I would need to take medications for life, but my God is a healer. And I am no longer worried about having someone in my life who only stays for a time. I enjoy people and the times and moments they journey with me. I have faith that when it is the right time, God will send the man who is meant for me, one who embodies the same virtues, values, morals, integrity, and character as I do, a man I will honor with my heart, admire, and relish with my affection. We will see; only God knows my plan and process, but I know I am prepared for whatever may come as he walks with me, as I learn my life's lessons.

As you can see, I have perfected my character as I have learned about others as well as myself. I have learned virtues and values and what is important to me. I have learned to be patient, to be peaceful, and to go with the flow of life, which is most likely what God wanted from me in the first place.

Great sites to look at if you are attempting to change your life for the better:

www.growinginchrist.com

The Joel Osteen site offers a wonderful article entitled *New Beginning*: http://www.joelosteen.com/Pages/Article. aspx?articleid=6482

I highly recommend you attend church and feed your spirit with the word, not only at church, but on your own free time. Learn as much as you can about anything that interests you. You are such a magnificent masterpiece! Believe in yourself and go be GREAT!

Thoughts and Reflections

Great books to read:

Woman, Thou Art Loosed, by T.D. Jakes
The Lady, Her Lover, and Her Lord, by *T.D. Jakes*
Live a Thousand Years, by Giovanni Livera
The Art of Abundance, by Candy Paull
Stilettos in the Kitchen, by Shanel Cooper-Sykes
Preparing to Be a Help Meet, by Debi Pearl

Printed in the United States
By Bookmasters